An Introduction to Scrum

Understanding and Applying the Software

By: Ted Owens

DEDICATION

If you need to learn Scrum or in fact any technology based system you need to start from the basics. Lots of techs won't tell you that before Geek there was Non-Geek. I was and still am a Non-Geek and so I dedicate this book to the Non Geeks out there trying to learn Scrum Agile Development!

"It has become appallingly obvious that our technology has exceeded our humanity."

- Albert Einstein.

TABLE OF CONTENTS

CHAPTER 1- SCRUM-THE BASICS

History

In its original context the word "scrum" is actually a rugby term. It refers to re-starting the game after there's been a minor infraction on the field. The concept was adapted and used in the world of software development in 1986. That was the year when Hirotaka Takeuchi first defined scrum as "a flexible, holistic product development strategy where a development team works as a unit to reach a common goal." Scrum was a new concept at the time, and it was in direct opposition to the older method which is usually referred to as the traditional, sequential approach to programming.

Software companies got the idea from studies in the automotive industry, as well as in printer and photocopier industries, where experiments had been done assembling a single, cross-discipline team to complete a single project. The approach was called the holistic approach, or the rugby approach, because the team would pass the ball back and forth with each member doing his or her part to reach the goal that had been set forth for them as a whole.

It took until the early 1990s for the idea of an adaptive, team approach to software development to be referred to as scrum. It was used at a company called Easel Corporation, and though the idea wasn't theirs alone they were the first company to use that particular 5-letter word to describe how they were managing their development teams. The term continued to grow in popularity, and it was solidified in place by the book Agile Software Development With Scrum, which was published in the year 2001. Since that time scrum and agile software development have been linked in the minds of programmers, as well as in the culture of the software design industry. In 2009 Scrum.org was founded by Ken Schwaber in an attempt to refine and improve on the ideas that he and his company had already helped create.

What Is Scrum?

To put it in plainer language, scrum was designed as a way to turn a software development team into a single, cohesive, organic unit which was focused on creating a program to fulfill a client's needs. Previously programming was more like an assembly line, where each individual would do his or her part, and then pass it along to the next programmer in line to handle. While making programming an assembly line was occasionally efficient, it didn't allow for the possibility that the client might change his or her mind, or that something would need to be re-thought or re-designed. That's why programming has moved to endorse the scrum style more than the traditional, sequential approach.

How Scrum Works

Most people have participated in a scrum style situation, even if they don't know it. Say that a client wants an app designed for her company. In order to put the project together the company would put together a number of specialists from a variety of disciplines, all of whom can come together to form a complete machine to produce the end product. The team will start each day with a face-to-face (or Skype, if in-person isn't possible) meeting where progress is discussed and the goals for the future are set up. Typically the team will also work in close proximity physically, and keep in contact electronically, so that any problems can be handled and fixed among the group. This helps speed up how quickly programs can be created, and it helps cut down on time for repairs and error correction.

Where the "starting over" part of it comes in is that sometimes the goals change when a software team is putting together a project. For instance, say that the client originally wanted an app to allow customers to find their stores, but now the customer has decided that a small, amusing game featuring the company mascot would be better. A scrum team can look at the work they've done so far, ask what can be salvaged, and scrap the rest to focus on the new goal. Because it's a small unit, and that small unit can respond much more quickly than an assembly line, even such a drastic change in focus can still be taken in stride and adjusted to with relatively little change in the workday.

Is Scrum Here to Stay?

While scrum has evolved since its creation nearly 30 years ago, it is still not a universal methodology. There are still companies, who use the traditional, incremental approach to create software, and they do so for a reason; often times it works just fine.

That's one of the untold stories of scrum's fairly brief history in the world of technology. It is faster, more adaptable, and results in a product that can change focus fairly quickly. However, scrum can also be fairly labor intensive, and it requires small islands of professionals to act together as teams to get the job done. Not every program requires that sort of setup, and there is still a case to be made for the incremental approach being used in a variety of different programming situations. In many cases it's easier, simpler, and cheaper when the programs being created don't require the intensive, small-unit tactics that a scrum approach delivers. Scrum is becoming the more dominant form of programming in many areas though, and for that reason it's gaining more and more attention.

With reams of reviews, thousands of pages of offline text, and a great deal of research done regarding scrum and its advantages, chances are good that it's going to remain the standard way that software designers provide product for their clients for some time to come. In fact scrum has spread beyond software, and it's become a model for how huge varieties of businesses now create products, handle production, and troubleshoot problems. As a solution it's adaptable and functional, and when a business finds something that works it will hang onto it until a better, and more profitable, solution comes along and makes itself known.

Chapter 2- The Scrum Framework

As an Agile software development project, most people will be interested in seeing what they can get from Scrum. This is a program that can actually help people get a holistic and entirely flexible approach to the way that they create content. Part of the appeal behind the program is that it does use a collaborative effort. Scrum has actually been created to help bring together teams during this process as well. Every team will need to be able to divvy up the work load, which will help people adjust to this process as well. Managers may need to take the initiative on this, since it may be complicated. They should make sure that they are familiarized with the way that these systems can work throughout the year as well.

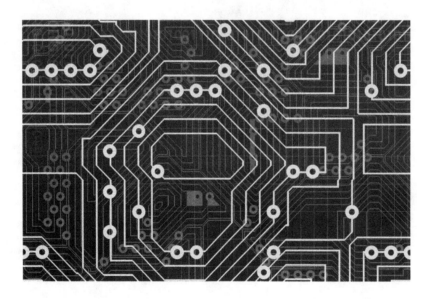

First, most teams will need to understand more about the roles that are assigned during this process. There are actually multiple different roles that people may play when they set up these different types of frameworks. They are loosely divided between core roles and ancillary roles. Those with core roles will be committed to seeing the project through until the end. Ancillary roles will typically be involved and may be sought after at different types of points as well. Almost everyone will appreciate that they can learn more information about how to upgrade their resources in just a short amount of time. Dividing up these roles can make it fairly simple for people to adjust to the way that these frameworks can be created throughout the year.

Most Scrum projects will require a team leader to step forward at some point. This leader is typically referred to as the Scrum Master, who can adapt to a few different types of challenges. This leader will need to be able to identify some of the different components of managing this process. Most people will be interested in learning more about how they can improve on these results as well. Ideally, the Scrum Master will have overseen these different types of projects in the past. This will prove to be an invaluable resource available to owners who need to learn more information quickly. This will be an important consideration for most owners to remember. They may want to attend a seminar training to get a primer on how these issues may best be managed as well.

Product owners will naturally want to get a time-fame estimate of when these projects will be completed. Fortunately, Scrum has been designed to accommodate these different types of requests. Everyone will be impressed by the sheer amount of resources that they have available to them as well. These times may actually be impacted by a few different variables. Manpower and on site resources will have an impact on the time frame of completion. Product owners will likely want to account for these variables if they want to learn more information about how this can work. This could prove to be an invaluable resource when people think about how they can accommodate this process. Most product owners will appreciate getting a time frame quote in just a short amount of time.

There are some specialized features that will help set Scrum apart from many other kinds of products out on the market. It does feature the sprint concept, which has proven to be highly effective over time. Most people will want to know how they can upgrade the different types of resources on the market. Sprints are typically time boxed, which means that they will be put in to place for just a short amount of time. This could prove to be an invaluable asset for most people out on the market. Nearly everyone will want to check out how they can customize the experience that they can find through here. Team members will likely need to be reminded that they will need to complete work within the parameters of this kind of event.

There are a few ways that users can actually identify some of the different solutions to the process that they are facing. Scrum will be ready to help people adapt to the different types of resources that they may face along the way. These projects are documented and user oriented, which will be an invaluable asset for most people in the community. Nearly everyone will appreciate that they can actually identify some of the core features associated with these products. This will help to make sure that owners are able to learn more about the resources that they can find during this process as well.

Every team member will likely want to stay updated on the artifacts that are included during this process. There are sprint backlogs, which will help team members stay up to date on the different types of projects that are due. In Chapter 4, I will discuss Sprints in greater detail. There are also product backlogs, which will help keep teams oriented towards these kinds of projects as well. Most owners will appreciate that they can actually learn more about these products going forward. Owners may want to schedule some frequent meetings, which can help people get updates on the way this works. This will be an invaluable resource for owners who are waiting for results to take place.

Ultimately, this will help people adapt to some of the different types of resources that they can find. This product software is surprisingly cost effective for teams to integrate. This can actually help owners adapt to different types of challenges that they may encounter throughout the year. Most people will want to acquire the resources that they can put things in to place soon. They can get a quote for the time and resources that a project may consume. This will combine to make it fairly effective to deal with different types of issues throughout the year. Most everyone will want to learn more about the functionality of their products. There are several testing phases that will make sense of the Scrum products being unveiled.

CHAPTER 3- AGILE PRINCIPLES- AN OVERVIEW

Agile is an umbrella term encompassing numerous methodologies (or implementations). Scrum is the most popularly-applied of these methodologies, accounting for over 80 percent of worldwide Agile implementation. In 2001, the Agile Manifesto established principles for the related movement that has arguably altered the world of software development.

Agile Principles As Stated In The Agile Manifesto:

The Agile principles are laid out in the Agile Manifesto drive "better ways of developing software". These twelve principles serve as the Bible for Agile practitioners around the world, and in whatever workplace where they might be found. As the best known of Agile methodologies, Scrum values also arise from this common basis.

1. "Our highest priority is to satisfy the customer through early and continuous delivery of valuable software." Premium is placed on jumping in, getting started developing software immediately, without waiting to create instruction manuals. Get useful software to the customer, responding as well as possible to requirements and needs—then making continuous improvement down the road to make it even more useful.

2. "Welcome changing requirements, even late in development. Agile processes harness change for the customer's competitive advantage." Rather than resenting the intrusion of changes in customer requirements, the approach is to not only expect them as a part of the process of software development, but to create a competitive advantage for the customer by exploiting them.

3. "Deliver working software frequently, from a couple of weeks to a couple of months, with a preference to the shorter timescale." No more the long-term development schedules for new software, the Agile emphasis is on getting the stuff to the customer quickly and often. This best gets the software where it can start delivering benefits, but also yields real-world application results—and related possibilities for improvement.

4. "Business people and developers must work together daily throughout the project." Only by working consistently in an iterative process with business people can software

developers know they are really delivering a product of the highest value to customers. Only by working side-by-side with developers can customers know their concerns are being addressed throughout, and their input being taken seriously.

5. "Build projects around motivated individuals. Give them the environment and support they need, and trust them to get the job done." Classic Theory Y over Theory X management, this value has been tested across industries and enterprise level. Here it receives a strong plug for application to the development of software.

6. "The most efficient and effective method of conveying information to and within a development team is face-to-face conversation." For a group of software development professionals living in the Internet Age, (who largely live their lives virtually), to place a high priority on face-to-face conversation for developing effective software, certainly confirms its importance. Firing angry e-mails back-and-forth, or communicating through Google Chat, just doesn't get the job done properly.

7. "Working software is the primary measure of progress." Cutting through all the rest of the activity that goes along with developing software—e.g., discussing, brainstorming, planning, manualizing, testing, revising—this principle places a premium on getting to the objective of all these. The point

of all this "progress" is to get the working software developed and in the hands of customers.

8. "Agile processes promote sustainable development. The sponsors, developers, and users should be able to maintain a constant pace indefinitely." A warning to obsessed, workaholic software developers everywhere, this ideal says essentially "nice and easy does it every time." A harried team of developers, exhausted and out of ideas, can hardly create the greatest good for their customers.

9. "Continuous attention to technical excellence and good design enhances agility." Ongoing learning with a focus on quality assures the most advanced (and best) software gets developed with the least mistakes.

10. "Simplicity—the art of maximizing the amount of work not done—is essential." "Simplicity is the ultimate sophistication" says Leonardo da Vinci, and he should know. And simplicity is often equated with genius. Here the ideal of simplicity is all about eliminating the extra effort that senseless complication can bring.

11. "The best architectures, requirements, and designs emerge from self-organizing teams." Self-organizing teams align themselves, firstly, in terms of compatible personalities and work patterns. That's important, without question. Even more critically, teams that organize themselves tend to emphasize a good mix of complementary skills necessary for the development of excellent software.

12.	"At regular intervals, the team reflects on how to become more effective, then tunes and adjusts its behavior accordingly." This corrective principle ensures that, in the process of developing useful software, the team pauses regularly to consider how they're doing. Working it into the schedule makes it more about process than emerging issues, or the (perhaps) jangled personalities involved.

What Agile Principles Mean For Scrum Values:

Like other Agile methodologies, successful Scrum application depends not only on trust in teams, but on the individuals in the teams and the way they interact. Teams figure out:

- What is to be done?
- How best it can be done.

Then teams actually do it. Scrum teams must produce an incremental product increment with every burst of organized effort, focusing on developing working software over meticulous documentation.

With Scrum, customer collaboration is more important than negotiating contracts. The product owner works collaboratively with the team to determine development priorities. All respond to change over sticking to a careful plan of work. Each member has the information he/she needs to make a practicable decision as necessary. Progress is visible; problems and issues are discussed openly.

Scrum Development Team Roles Promote These Values:

Every member of a scrum software development team brings these values to life during the course of the project. Clearly the product owner, who must be a single person, behaves as a manager—but he has other individuals to support his direction efforts. These individuals are:

- **Development team members:** Cross-functional professionals do the work of delivering the product.
- **ScrumMaster:** "Servant leader" who trains others in subtleties of the framework and removing impediments to progress.

The ScrumMaster fosters team self-organization too, meaning the team itself addresses impediments when possible.

CHAPTER 4- SPRINTS- WHAT ARE THEY AND HOW DO THEY WORK?

Scrum might seem like an odd choice of wording to describe something related to software. When the word scrum is associated with sprinting, people may have an even more quizzical look on their faces. The average person does not really have a need to know what scrum refers to; nor does the average person need to know what scrum sprinting is or how it works.

The Path To Understanding How Scrum Works

If you are someone looking for information on the topic of scrum, then it is safe to say you are not exactly the average person. You likely have a pressing need to know what this concept refers to since it likely relates to you and your profession. Learning the basics of what scrum is, what its related sprints are and how they work just might make a host of your daily tasks easier.

Not everyone is technologically savvy nor is the average person a master of software program. However, people of all walks of life do have to work with technology and software in some capacity. Those who are in business do have to take the time out to expand their knowledge on these topics. The following is a brief look at scrum and its related sprinting. Hopefully, the information presented will offer reliable insight.

Scrum As A Software Component

The best way to describe scrum is to call it exactly what it is, an Agile software development framework. Specifically, it is an iterative and incremental Agile framework. The purpose of scrum is rather straight forward. The program seeks to manage software projects and also manage the development of a product or an application. The next question that emerges here is, what is a sprint and how does it connect to scrum development?

Sprints Examined From A Scrum Perspective

A sprint is rather easy to comprehend. As mentioned in Chapter 2, Sprint is a set period of duration in which specific defined work must be completed. Once it has been completed, then the work is ready for review. Since scrum entails the production and management of products and applications,

Another way of describing a sprint is the more technical term, iteration (Sprinting can be deemed a colloquial means of defining the term). In a scrum sprint, work is locked into a particular cycle. The sprint cycle is both regular and repeatable. There is a common duration for a sprint, but it is not universal across all projects. In general, a sprint will run about 30 days although short sprint cycles certainly can be possible as well. One, two, or three week cycles would be these shorter durations.

The length of the cycle has to be thought out carefully and deliberately. Each individual team must arrive at the right sprint cycle based on a detailed analysis of what the pros and cons of a particular cycle are. A long sprint cycle might have quite a few benefits, but it also may have disadvantages. The same can, of course, be said about the shorter sprint cycles. Each and every development environment is going to be different, which is why careful thought has to go into the selection of an actual duration cycle. A point that does have to be clearly and definitively stressed here is there must be a consistent duration cycle with a sprint.

Those In Charge Of The Scrum Sprinting

The creation of a sprint all starts with a planning meeting. The person who is requesting the product being developed has to be at the meeting in order to articulate what he/she needs done and why. This returns us to the previous point about why it is necessary to be at least minimally knowledgeable about certain software and technology topics. The person requesting the product does have to at least be somewhat aware of what the development process is going to entail. If not, then the meeting might never end up being as productive as it needs to be.

The product owner requesting the work is going to be making the request of a skilled development team. The one thing that clearly has to be agreed upon during the meeting is the type of work that is to be accomplished during the sprint. No ambiguity should be present here at all since a lack of clarity is going to do little more than create major problems during the actual sprint cycle.

The product requester does have to accept a few basic facts when sitting in on these meetings. For one, it is the development team that has the final say on how the sprint cycle will work. While it is true the person making the request is likely, for all intents and purposes, the boss of the operation as I said in Chapter 3, he or she is not exactly technically savvy about how to create a scrum sprint and what exactly has to be specifically done during the sprint cycle. Only what is feasible should be performed and those on the development team are the only ones capable of making such an assessment.

Granted, the product requester is always going to be the person who has the final say in terms of giving the go ahead to have the scrum sprint cycle launched. Approval has to come from someone and that someone is always going to be the person who approves and accepts a work proposal.

The duration of the approved sprint will be set forth by the scrum master though. As the facilitator of the team, he/she works with the team to figure out how many days the sprints should be. Again, all future sprints have to be the same duration (30 days or less) in order to maintain consistency.

The scrum sprinting process is not all that complicated to understand. Now, the actual process of designing the sprint can be complex to execute, this is a task left to the design team. For the person who is requesting the work, all that is required, is having a basic, simple understanding of the work to be done.

CHAPTER 5- USER STORIES AND REQUIREMENTS SCRUM

A user story is a software specification requirement. These are quick ways to manage end user requirements without having to draw up lots of formal documents. The stories can also quickly respond to changing requirements. User stories are used at the start of the project, although as iterations are performed the stories may be changed.

In software development, user stories define what should be built into the project. It describes the functionality that will be useful to the end-user, or the purchaser of a software system. Although, typically user stories chronicle a fast-moving process, they often are like short notes written on post-it cards.

Creating User Stories

When the time comes to create user stories, one of the developers will meet with the client's representative. The developer will use a series of questions so that the client will ask about the appropriateness of some particular functions. Here is where you'll capture the "who", "what" and "why" in a concise way, but the developer must be careful not to dominate the creation process.

Features Of A User Story

User stories should be:

Independent of each other: If necessary, combine the dependent stories or find another way to divide the stories so that they are independent.

Descriptive Notes: The story itself is not sufficiently explicit to be considered a contract, the discussion should allow users to clarify its scope and it should be left in the form of explicit validation tests.

Estimable: Feels a bit like you're reading a crystal ball, but you should be able to measure the time it will take to complete. As a result of the team discussion and client communication, you develop a timeline, i.e., total project time.

Small: Very long stories are difficult to estimate and impose restrictions on planning an iterative development. Consolidation of very short stories is usually recommended for each user story.

The user story should answer three questions:

- Who benefits?
- What do you want?
- What is the benefit?

Therefore, some authors recommend writing user stories in this format:

- As a (role) I want (something) to (benefit).

By definition, user stories are usually not, and should not have the level of detail that often is found in requirement specifications. A user story should be small with the ability to memorize, and could be developed quickly by a couple of programmers. This is why it's often recommended that you draft user stories in short sentences or the particular format previously mentioned.

User stories have great functionality. Take, for example, the following case history that perfectly illustrates the structure and behavior of a user story:

- Role: literary critic
- I want to: read a book
- To Benefit: write a review for the book

These three elements form the core of every user story. In the first (Role) is established who the user or user group is and how to 'intervene'; typically a user role in the development of this software responds to the question "Who will use the functionality" described by this story.

The second element (Do) is the activity, the focus of the story, what the user does in the story. And the third element (To Benefit) is the purpose of the story, the goal you want to achieve. All these collectively describe a purpose. It is generally accepted that the estimated time of completion is between 10 hours and a few weeks. Estimates older than two weeks are an indication that the story is very complex and should be divided into several stories.

Effective Use

As a central part of many agile development processes user stories define what has to be built into the software project. User stories are prioritized by the client to indicate the most important requirements to the system and then is divided into tasks and completion estimated by the developers.

Each user story should eventually have one or more tests run, which allows the developer to test when the user story is complete and also allows the customer to validate it. Some characteristics of the user stories include:

1. They are short and easy to read.
2. Understandable by developers, Stakeholders and users.

3. Represent small increments of functions which can be developed over a period of days or weeks

The user story is more of an informal statement of your obligation. Before a user story is implemented appropriate acceptance procedure must be written by the customer to ensure by testing or otherwise if you have met the objectives of the user story. The meeting of the minds finally occurs when the user story is accepted thus creating a specific work order.

Scrum

Scrum is used to resolve situations where you're not giving the customer what they need, or when deliveries are too long, costs are skyrocketing and the quality is not acceptable.

Scrum acts as the project plan with a list of objectives or requirements. As you learned in Chapter 1, scrum is a process that regularly applies a set of best practices for working collaboratively as a team to get the best possible outcome. Scrum helps prioritize and put the focus on selecting the most important things to do first.

There is a list of objectives or prioritized product requirements which act as the project plan.

60 % of project problems are caused directly or indirectly in the requirements, and the problems typically arise for any of these reasons:

1. The client does not have a clear vision.

2. The supplier obtains the requirements superficially, perhaps following a process, but without "diving" in knowing the client's business and then performing the analysis.

3. Internal communication problems with the client development team.

The best solution to solve project problems is by integrating more participation in the development process and more detailed client communication.

There are some limitations of the user stories. They can be difficult to scale for large projects and user stories are only considered topics of conversation to meet small requirements, but not meant for complex projects.

CHAPTER 6- DEALING WITH PRODUCT BACKLOG IN SCRUM

Manage Product Backlog In Scrum

Scrum organizes your resources for understanding the end result and the big picture while allowing your development team to focus on the necessary tasks. Scrum brings the end user into the process via stories as you saw in the previous chapter, and the product backlog manages those stories and keeps those stakeholders involved and informed. The product backlog prioritizes all your deliverables, organizes your development team, and communicates clear goals to the end users. Since it brings the needs of the end users and customer into your development team's processes, it can be useful for adding value to your business. As your backlog helps order and assign value to your priorities, you also establish a systematic, transparent method for adding value, maximizing profit and delivering the best product.

Human Capital: Using Product Backlog To Enable And Organize A Development Team

Many teams create the product backlog with user stories entirely, under the assumption that this is the best way to identify and organize end users' ideas and requirements. You can also use a project roadmap or a vision board. However you manage the project, though, use the product backlog as the major resource for your development team.

It's more than just a list of items. Your team should meet regularly to workshop items at a very large scale, eventually breaking down items to the very fine grain necessary for the next phase. In these big-scope meetings, you will discover how and why you need to update the backlog. For example, outside market forces may cause you to change items, or end user feedback. Of course, you will often have more backlog items that your team can properly move forward. As you prioritize your items, they become progressively more refined. As you refine and add detail, those items can be handed off to the delivery team. Remember your DEEP acronym: "detailed appropriately, emergent, estimated and prioritized [or, as is more commonly said now, "ordered"]". Your development team will ensure that any item close to the top of your backlog should be testable and clearly stated.

As your project begins to scale up, your Scrum methods will help run several teams working together on the same project. Use the product backlog to emphasize transparency and quality.

Promote Product Backlog As A Way To Identify And Prioritize Customer Needs

The product backlog increases efficiencies by showing when and why the end user or customer may have updated a need. The business can balance this against the overall impact of the project. Managing customer expectations, while incorporating their changing wants is extremely important. The agile "mindset" allows you to be accommodating while maintain quality. Your customer is engaged throughout the process, and in many instances, is a very important part of the process. Note: you will be required to "groom" the backlog to keep it in working order. A bloated backlog of ideas no one is clear on, or committed to, is a sure way to frustrate everyone. Spend no more than 10% of your team's time grooming your backlog to remove the ideas you won't deliver. Use a template to move items around easily and keep track of everything.

Maximize Product Backlog To Maximize Profit

As you, your customer, and your product owner make choices about how to prioritize items in your backlog, you usually use business benefit and cost to weigh your choices. This allows you to create a coherent way of evaluating business benefits. A product owner can estimate any item before it's ordered. The development team can add an estimated cost. These figures give some data for creating a process for prioritizing all items. Additionally, you are able to manage your teams better, control costs, anticipate new needs and understand how your product will fare in the overall market context. Through the backlog, you have data on all activity, so you can determine where production can be increased.

Understand Product Backlog As A Resource For All Strategic Communications

Given that your product will change throughout the course of development, it is imperative to keep everyone updated on the product's evolution. A product backlog is best used as a living document, as your customer needs may change, your user stories will reorganize in priority and your team moves into different work stages. Use the product backlog to structure your communications in order to keep all your stakeholders informed without giving anyone too much confusing detail. You can even make the product backlog visible to all stakeholders. Scrum is built on responsiveness and transparency. Use the project backlog to emphasize care and interest in everyone's needs.

Develop The Very Best Product With The Product Backlog

The reason we're all here is to produce the highest value product. The product backlog enhances your final product because within Agile, both the product and the foundational code are important to everyone. By emphasizing intentional cross-functionality and real collaboration, the product backlog maximizes your product as well as your human resources and your relationship with your customer.

Using Scrum, the process itself becomes part of the product, or experience, in a very important way. Of course, the product backlog gives you the tools to identify and build the most valuable products first. But it also shows the entire group and your customers where all the items fit into your overall plan, so it eliminates anxiety around those items which are not currently part of your flow. This is related to both your strategies for communications and for human resource management: if every team member and end user can see where his/her priorities fall on your workflow, you've taken a big step toward meeting needs in a quantifiable way.

Within your Scrum framework, a challenge can always be framed as an opportunity, and every opportunity can be examined for success for both business and customer. The methods of planning, communicating, prioritizing and delivering all add up to the best possible product. Use Scrum and the backlog for a healthy process and a great product.

Chapter 7- What Are The Various Roles Of Scrum Team Members?

When it comes to the various roles of Scrum team members, the thing to understand is that there are three distinct different roles when it comes to this. Scrum is a framework people use to build a product using a more effective method. In general, the product will typically be built using incrementally short periods of time. These short periods are often referred to as sprints. A sprint refers to a fixed time period, and it will generally go up to four weeks, but usually, it is preferred if the increments are shorter than four weeks.

Each sprint will focus on one aspect of a product. During this sprint, the team will build and deliver that aspect of the product.

The Product Owner

The product owner on a Scrum team is a mix between a traditional product manager and a project sponsor. However, the product owner will have a lot more interaction with the development team. When it comes to the role of a product owner, he/she has the responsibility of deciding what work is to be done. He/she also has a responsibility for bringing forth the most valuable product at the end of the deadline.

As product owner, he/she has a responsibility to manage the flow of work that is being given to the team. Also, he/she will select and improve the items that are found on the backlog. The product owner also maintains the product backlog and will ensure that everyone knows what their responsibilities are and what the priorities are. The product owner can be supported by other people, but there cannot be multiple product owners. A product owner will be the individual who works the closest with the business aspect of the project.

Scrum Master

A Scrum Master oversees the process. He/she is the process referee, and he/she ensures that the methodology for the product has been followed. Another role the Scrum master will take on is being responsible for coaching the team, and he/she will also figure out how to make the most of the Scrum's processes and artifacts to maximize the product.

As mentioned in Chapter 3, the best word to describe a Scrum Master would be a servant leader. His responsibility will be to help the rest of the Scrum team follow the process. In order to be an efficient Scrum Master, he must have a thorough understanding of the Scrum framework, and he has to be able to train others in the subtleties. In addition, a Scrum Master also helps the product owner understand the process for creating and maintaining the product backlog. Also, he will be required to find and implement technical practices that help to get the job done after each sprint.

Another one of the responsibilities that the Scrum Master has is to find and remove anything that might be impeding the team's progress. These conflicts could include internal conflicts or external conflicts. For example, it could be two team members who do not get along, and they are slowing down the progress. The Scrum Master can create meetings, and he always plays the role of the coach for the rest of the Scrum team. He will also help team members collaborate more efficiently and learn the framework that is Scrum. Scrum Master ensures that the Scrum team does not go off track, and he ensures they grow in ability and that they stay productive. Finally, the Scrum Master will help everyone to improve because this makes the Scrum team more valuable, and it ensures that the best product possible will be given.

The Development Team

The development team will develop the product. They will be a group that can self-organize, and they will be a cross-functional group. They deliver the skills necessary to reach the goals for the product. As a development team, they will be doing the legwork of the project, and they will deliver the product increments. The group will be cross-functional in the sense that the people of the group will have all the necessary skills for delivering each increment for the product. They also have the responsibility for self-organizing in order to accomplish each sprint goal. A development team will produce each new product increment according to the sprint plan. Once the product owner has made an ordered list of what needs to be done, the development team will give the product owner an estimation of how much they will be able to accomplish in a single sprint. The development team also decides how they will go about creating the increment of each product for each sprint.

Each team member will have to be focused in order to accomplish goals. They should also be open to learning new methods because this helps to make them more efficient. As a team, they will also display a commitment to one another because this ensures that the product gets the job done in a manner that is quickest and most efficient. Also, commitment to the project ensures that the product gets developed by the deadline that has been listed. Not just a product that gets developed by the deadline, but it ensures that the best product gets developed by the deadline. Courage of the team should also be displayed because in order to truly create a product that thinks outside of the box, it requires a team that is willing to take calculated risks to find the best way to develop a valuable product.

When it comes to Scrum, there are three essential artifacts: The Product Increment, the Product Backlog and the Sprint Backlog. These artifacts are there to ensure that the product runs smoothly and that everything goes according to plan. What's more, it helps to ensure that the team knows what they are creating and what they should be doing. These are all things that will make a big difference in the long term. The various roles of Scrum team members are important because it ensures that everyone knows what he/she should be doing. It ensures that the best product possible is made.

ABOUT THE AUTHOR

Ted Owens is an economist but had an interest in learning about software development programs. Scrum was something that he had been interested in since it was launched in 1986. From what he learned, he thought that others would also be interested in learning about the benefits of scrum.

Ted started to compile a book on scrum with that in mind. He shows how scrum allows a group of persons to work on a project as a unit. He has used it himself with other team members and has found it to be quite effective.